SPORTS
ACTIVITY BOOK

Becky Radtke

D1392150

DOVER PUBLICATIONS, INC.
Mineola, New York

Bibliographical Note

Sports Activity Book is a new work, first published by Dover Publications, Inc., in 1998.

International Standard Book Number: 0-486-40303-3

Manufactured in the United States of America
Dover Publications, Inc., 31 East 2nd Street, Mineola, N.Y. 11501

Note

Hey, young sports fans, check out this cool collection of crosswords, word searches, mazes, and dot-to-dot activities. Each puzzle is based on a favorite sport including baseball, basketball, hockey, and soccer. Carry this handy little volume wherever you go, in your backpack or pocket. Grab some pencils or crayons, and put on your thinking cap. Solve the puzzles, and color them in, too. If you get stumped, the answers begin on page 52. But don't peek too soon. It may take you a few minutes to come up with a solution—but it's so much more fun.

Stand on this and take a ride,
Learn to zigzag from side to side!
Connect the dots to see what it is.

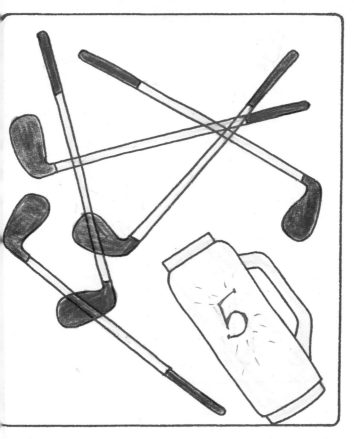

Oops! Someone has spilled this bag of golf clubs.
How many do you count in the jumble above?
Write the number on the bag.

5

s o c c e r

b a s k e t b a l l

p a d d l i n g

Use the picture clues to sound out the names of some popular sports. Write the words in the blanks.

1—red   2—yellow   3—blue

Michelle is ready to play volleyball. Follow the number code to color her uniform.

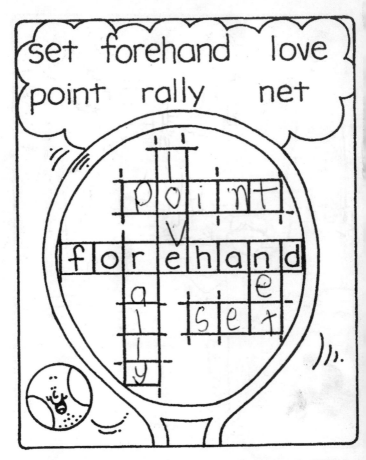

set forehand love
point rally net

If you play tennis, you might know these words. Write them in the correct places in this racquet.

8

1–He is smiling. 2–He is waving. 3–He is holding a towel.

Use the clues to figure out which swimmer has won the 200 meter race. Circle him.

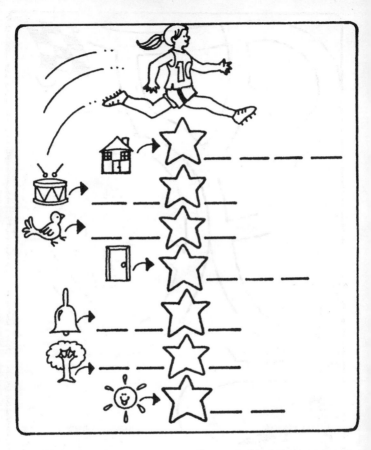

When you write the name of each picture you will find out what runners leap over. The answer is in the stars.

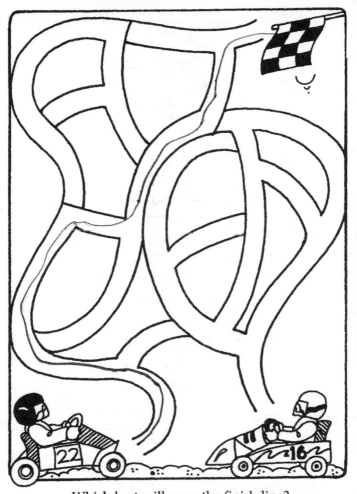

Which kart will cross the finish line?

Count how many times this crowd has yelled,
"Go Team!" Write the number on the pennant.

10

Unscramble these pins to spell something everybody likes to get when they bowl.

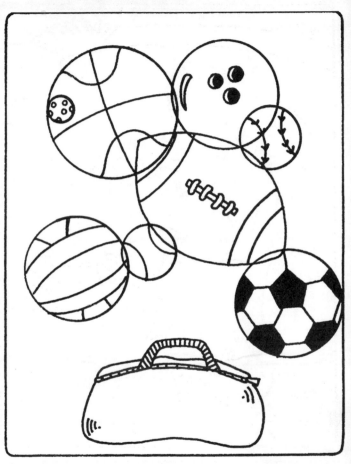

How many balls can you count? Write the number on the sports bag at the bottom of the picture.

Circle the running shoe that is different from the others.

Season Ticket

coat

_____ _____

_____ _____

_____ _____

_____ _____

_____ _____

_____ _____

_____ _____

How many words can you spell using the letters on this ticket? One word has already been written for you.

SWOBLE

_ _ _ _ _ _

SEENK

_ _ _ _ _

These words are written backward. Write them forward in the blanks to find out what body parts you should protect with pads when you skateboard.

A referee, or sports official, makes decisions during a game about how the players are following the rules. Circle the referee's shirt.

Draw three things in the top picture so it will
look just like the bottom one.

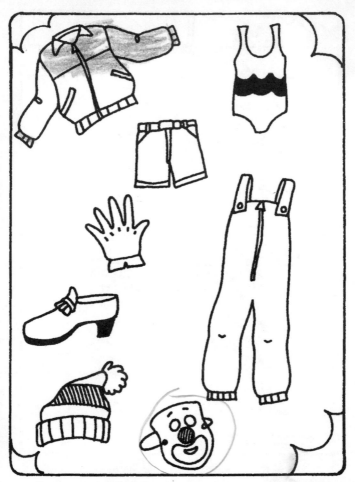

Circle everything you would wear when you ski.

These two pictures are almost the same. Circle three things that are different in the bottom picture.

Jane is a terrific baseball player! Put the balls in their correct number order to find out which base she is running to.

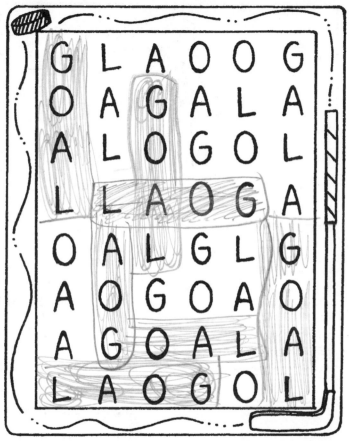

It's an exciting, high scoring hockey game. Find and circle the word "goal" which has been written seven times in the rink. Look up, down, foreward, and back.

Write the first letter of each picture in the box below it to find out where you go bowling.

24

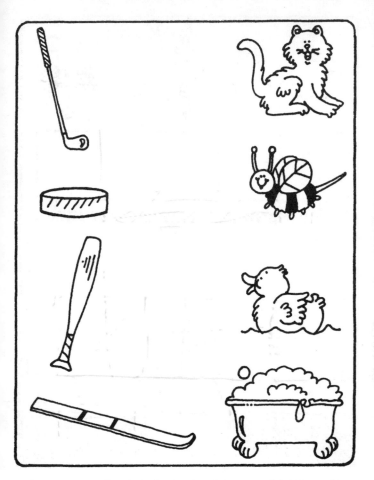

Draw a line from each sports object on the left to the word it rhymes with on the right.

25

tumble leap
bend hop
balance jump

Q	T	S	J	I	W	B
H	B	U	L	U	P	X
O	D	L	M	V	M	O
P	N	Z	F	B	H	P
K	S	E	O	E	L	A
B	A	L	A	N	C	E
T	A	Y	J	D	K	L

Find the words above in the puzzle. They are all activities done by a gymnast.

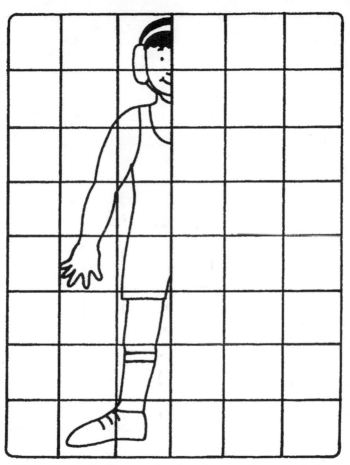

Wayne wants to wrestle, but he needs your help. Finish his other half so he can start his match. Use the lines of the grid as a guide. 27

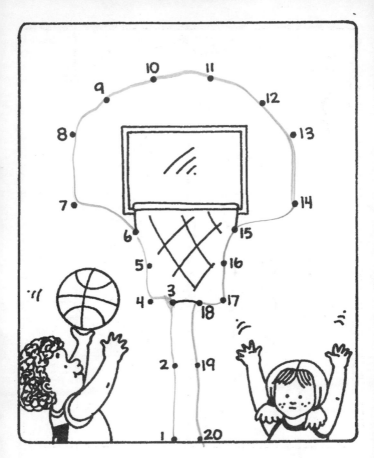

This is where the player wants his basket to go in.
If he dunks the ball many times, his team might win!
Connect the dots to see what it is.

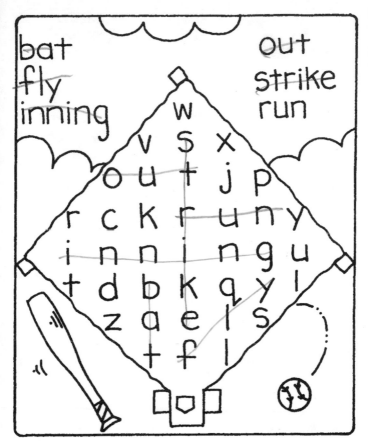

bat
fly
inning

out
strike
run

Find and circle the words about baseball that are hidden on the diamond.
Look up, down, across, and on the diagonal.

29

s p s a

_ _ _ _

i k k c

_ _ _ _

r a t p

_ _ _ _

Unscramble the letters to find out what every soccer player should learn.

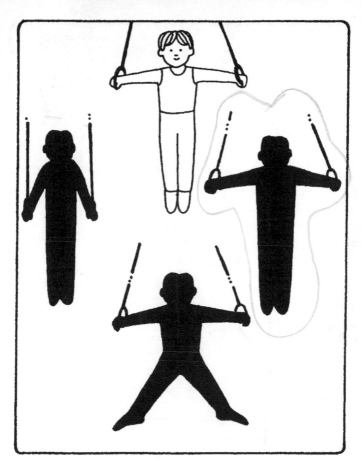

Victor, a strong gymnast, is working on the rings. Pick and circle his correct shadow.

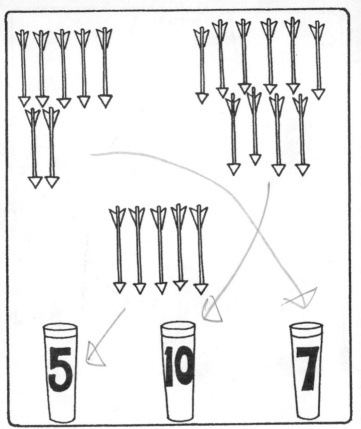

It's time to practice for the archery tournament. Count each bunch of arrows. Draw a line from each group to the quiver that has the matching number.

What should Angie wear on her feet to play hockey?
Draw a square around them.

Help the skier find the clear trail down the mountain.

Start at the bold "H" and follow the arrows to find out what Bobby hit when he was up at bat. Fill in the blanks with each letter on the path, in order.

Think of an original team logo and draw it on
36   the helmet below. Color it however you like.

Uh oh! Someone has lost five golf balls on this course. Can you spot all of them?

Follow the line from each girl to find out which diving board she will use.

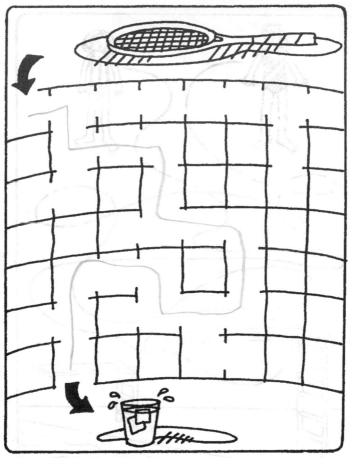

Hooray! You've just won a tennis match! Now find your way through the net to reach the glass of ice water.

Choose the one letter that will complete all of these words. Each completed word is something you can do during a volleyball match.

When a basketball player runs or walks with the ball, it's a foul. The referee has a special name for it. Find out what it is by using the code to fill in the letters. 41

Draw lines to connect the matching halves
of the barbells.

Add up the points on the clipboard of each coach.
Then, circle the winning score.

Surf's up! Find the banana, pencil, fish, octopus, and ice cream cone hidden in the waves.

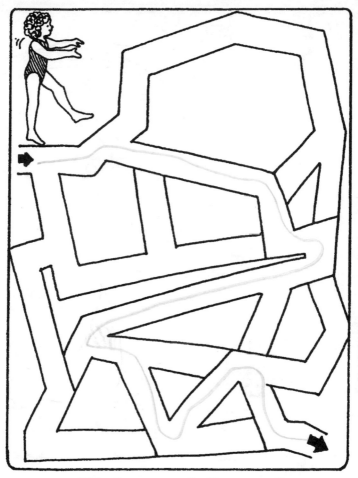

Help the gymnast find her way off
this wacky balance beam.

Following the three easy steps, use the empty
space on this page to draw a wind surfer.

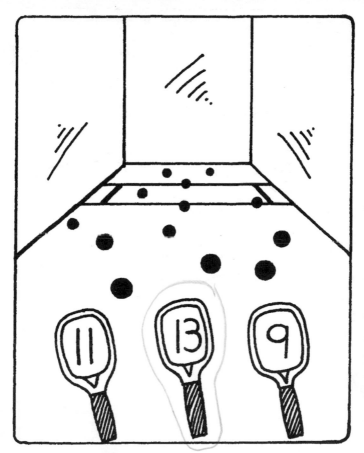

Someone has been practicing racquetball. Count the number of balls left on the court. Then, circle the racquet that has that number on it.

What does a football player make when he crosses the goal line with the ball? To find the answer, put an "X" on the first helmet and every other one after that. Write the remaining letters in the blanks.

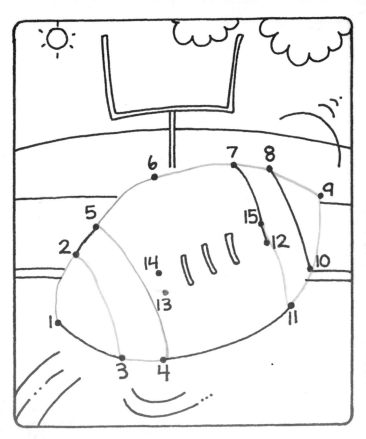

Look at what's spinning and passing by.
Will it make a touchdown when it falls from the sky?
Connect the dots to find out what it is.

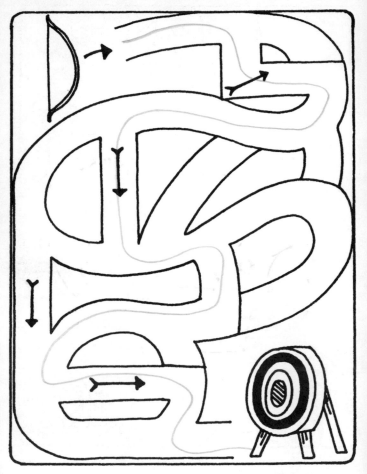

Begin at the bow. Travel to pick up each arrow.
End on the target.

Fill in the blanks with the letter "o" to find out what you should always be when you play a game.

Solutions

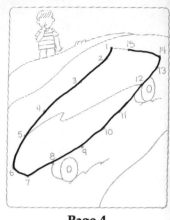

Page 4

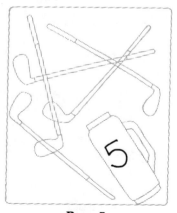

Page 5

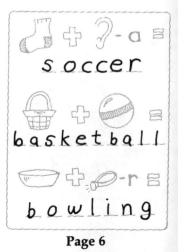

soccer

basketball

bowling

Page 6

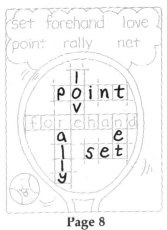

Page 8

Page 9

house
drum
bird
door
bell
tree
sun

Page 10

Page 11

53

Page 12

Page 13

Page 14

Page 15

coat	son
oat	ton
on	tin
it	take
at	tent
sat	sent
sit	eat
cake	seat

Page 16

SWOBLE
E L B O W S

SEENK
K N E E S

Page 17

Page 18

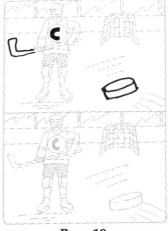

Page 19

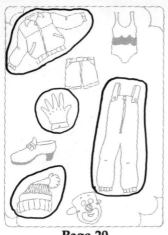

Page 20

Page 21

Page 22

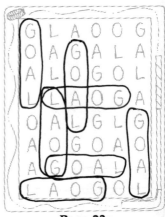

Page 23

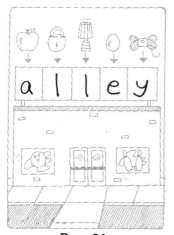

Page 24

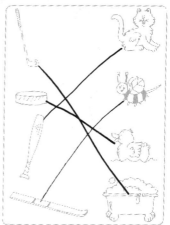

Page 25

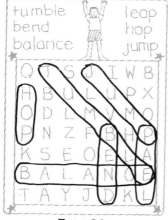

Page 26

Page 28

57

Page 29

Page 30

Page 31

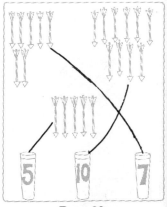

Page 32

58

Page 33

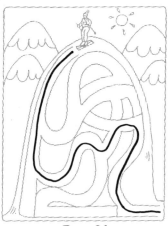

Page 34

Homerun

Page 35

Page 37

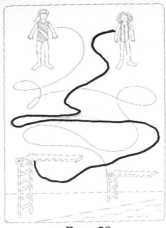

Page 38

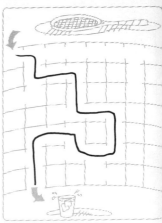

Page 39

Page 40

Page 41

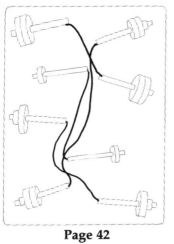

Page 42

Page 43

Page 44

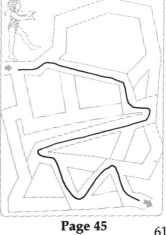

Page 45

61

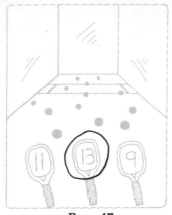

Page 47

t o u c h d o w n

Page 48

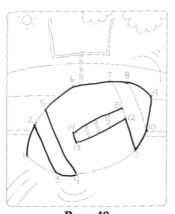

Page 49

Page 50

Page 51